Turnover, Mobility & Talent Upgrading

Steffen Parratt

Steffen Parratt

Copyright © 2013 Steffen Parratt
All rights reserved.
ISBN-10: 1493636898
ISBN-13: 978-1493636891

Turnover, Mobility & Talent Upgrading

Introduction	1
Turnover	3
Mobility	23
Talent Upgrading	29
Conclusion	31
Notes	33

Steffen Parratt

Introduction

Turnover, mobility and talent upgrading are three issues that all companies face periodically. Turnover may be a persistent drag on the firm, or it may rear its head after a crisis, a move by a competitor, or a management change. Mobility, which is the movement of employees within a firm, is a hot topic when several important positions are vacated, which managers scramble to fill by shuffling around employees. Talent upgrading often comes up after annual performance reviews, when managers realize their low performers remain entrenched.

The truth is that these three topics are directly related and need to be addressed as a single process. Disciplined talent upgrading leads to open positions within a firm. Mobility planning leads to a set of career-enhancing employee moves to fill those positions, often followed by an infusion of talent into the firm, all of which leads to good turnover. This book describes a unified approach to turnover, mobility and talent upgrading, and how it can raise the overall talent of an organization.

About this book

This is the *Turnover, Mobility & Talent Upgrading* volume of our "Single Sitting Simplification Series"

- Single Sitting – leaders are busy and do not have the time to read management tomes. Each volume of the series can be read within a single sitting, maybe over lunch, or on the train ride home.

- Simplification – this is not an exposition of new ideas in the theory of management. Instead, it is an aggregation of principles and practices relevant to talent management.

- Series – this one of a series of volumes that addresses the major topics relevant to leading a company.

It is a brief book, to the point, something that you carry around with you, scribbling in the margins, until you have completed the job. We are passionate about simplification; we have authored a simple book.

Turnover

Quantitative research has substantiated what practicing managers have always known intuitively – a moderate rate of employee turnover is desirable and improves the overall performance of an organization.[1,2] The figure below illustrates this relationship.[3] For this relationship to hold, the turnover must meet

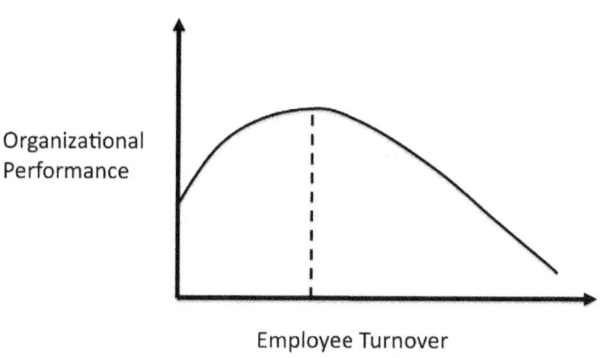

certain conditions and is thereby designated as "good" turnover.

Employee *turnover* is defined as the annual rate at which departing employees are replaced.[4] For example, if 5% of a company's employees depart during the year and are replaced with new employees, then the turnover rate is 5%. Turnover includes employees who leave voluntarily for other opportunities, as well as employees dismissed. Turnover does not include employees who move within a firm; *mobility* measures internal employee moves. Turnover and mobility can vary from year to year; the long-term average rate and its volatility are important metrics.

In this section we will discuss the following topics:

- What constitutes "good" turnover,
- Why moderate good turnover improves performance,
- Appropriate measures of good turnover, and
- How to encourage good turnover in an organization.

What constitutes good turnover

The overall rate of employee turner by itself tells very little about what is happening in an organization. For example, if a company has 5% turnover, that can be a good thing (if it represents the lowest performers in the firm) or a bad thing (if it represents the best performers). When we say that moderate turnover can help an organization, we mean moderate *good turnover*. To facilitate our discussion of good turnover, we use the example below.

Turnover, Mobility & Talent Upgrading

A senior member of a company's management team (Senior Mgr 4) has had steadily decreasing performance, and is now exiting the firm. His departure sets off a chain reaction of moves within the company and an infusion of talent into the company, as shown by the ovals and arrows. First, his position needs to be filled, either by the best manager from a lateral position, from the tier below, or through an outside hire. If it is a manager from the tier below, it could be one of his direct reports, or a manager reporting to one of his peers.

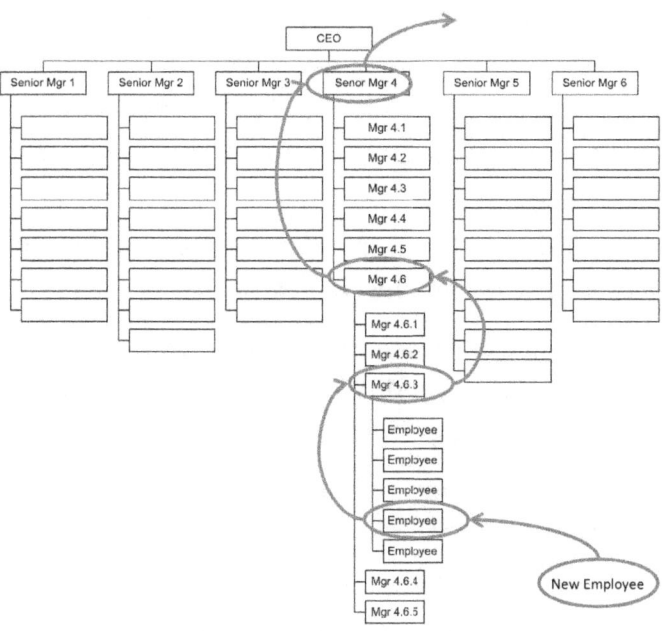

Let's assume the best candidate is Mgr 4.6 who is currently reporting to Senior Mgr 4. In turn, Mgr 4.6's position needs to be filled by an internal or external person, and, so on, down the chain. A talented new employee replaces the promoted employee at the bottom of the chain.

This case exhibits the hallmarks of good turnover: a poor performer was managed out of the firm, which led to internal upward mobility for several of the best managers and employees, followed by an infusion of talent into the firm.

Good turnover may vary based on the type of organization, its industry, and its business model. However, generally speaking, good turnover can be recognized as follows:

- The employees leaving the firm are the ones you want to leave. They are generally the lowest performing employees or are those no longer needed by the firm,
- The employees entering the organization are of a higher quality and better suited to the firm than those who are leaving,
- The turnover is distributed uniformly throughout the firm and at the different levels of the firm, and
- The turnover is stable over time.

Turnover, Mobility & Talent Upgrading

A firm with a disciplined performance rating system can identify its lowest performers annually. Ideally, those employees will be the ones leaving the firm each year; they are the least valuable employees to the firm and their departure can be anticipated and coordinated efficiently. However, the list of departing employees may also be studded with star employees with sparkling performance evaluations. These employees may be on the departure list for a good reason – they no longer fit within the firm, which may be for many reasons. For example, they may work in a country that the company is exiting. When judging the quality of turnover, consider employee performance ratings, but also employee division, function, and region, which may flag special circumstances.

Turning to our second condition for good turnover, entering employees should be of a higher quality than departing employees. At first blush this requirement may seem unreasonably difficult to measure. Clearly it is not practical to do a side-by-side comparison of each departing and entering employee. Frequently the employees entering and leaving are not even remotely equivalent. For example, turning back to our case study, the outgoing person (Senior

Mgr 4) and the incoming person (New Employee) do not fill the same role – how could we do a quality comparison in this case? Fortunately there is an easier and more reliable way to measure the relative quality of departing and entering employees.

Consider a hypothetical firm that annually identifies its 10% lowest performers and strongly encourages them to leave the firm. These employees are recognized by their performance ratings of "1", as opposed to the high-performers with ratings of "5", with all other employees somewhere in between. Let's assume that there is a long list of excellent candidates who wish to join the firm. While it is seldom easy or inexpensive to purge low performers, it is well worth the effort for a dramatic improvement in talent. An organization replacing low performers with high performers will make that effort and, as a result, there will be few employees in the organization with a history of "1" performance ratings for more than one or two years. That is, firms with few employees with a history of 1 performance ratings are upgrading their talent.

Now let us examine the opposite case. Let's assume that there is a dearth of excellent external candidates who wish to join the firm. In fact, let's assume that many of the candidates don't seem much better than the 10% low performing employees who received a 1 rating. It is unlikely that the firm will spend the effort and money to force out their low performers, just to hire and train candidates who seem quite similar. This firm will likely have many employees with a history of a 1 performance rating because the firm is not able to upgrade its talent.

The third condition for good turnover is that it is distributed uniformly throughout the firm. This is where reporting only average turnover can be deceptive. If most of the turnover is in one division, one region, or one level of the firm, then the average turnover rate may be fine, but the firm is not fine. This situation suggests a low-turnover firm with pockets of high turnover, both of which are unhealthy, which average out to look like a healthy firm. When evaluating the quality of turnover, we must examine each division, function, region and level of the firm.

The final condition for good turnover is that it is stable over time. Wild swings between low and high turnover may average out to a reasonable long-term rate, but the swings are not healthy. Furthermore, as we will see shortly, moderate turnover leads to healthy development of the experience base of its managers. Large exoduses and infusions of talent wipe out layers of developing managers and upset that developmental experience.

As we will discuss later, when creating a measurement and analysis capability for your firm, it is imperative that you identify and measure the underlying components of turnover to ensure that your average turnover rates are not masking serious underlying issues.

Why moderate good turnover improves organization performance

Let's revisit the turnover-performance curve shown at start of this chapter, beginning on the left-hand side. This graph suggests that firms with no employee turnover do not perform at their peak level (shown by the dashed line). A complete lack of turnover means that the lowest performing employees are not leaving the organization and are not being replaced by better performers. Employees leave even the best firms, and for many reasons: their interests change, opportunities arise elsewhere, they don't adapt to a changing landscape, they become too comfortable and no longer contribute at the level required, they choose not to physically relocate with the firm, the firm changes its focus, and so on.

Turnover, Mobility & Talent Upgrading

Low turnover causes all types of issues for a firm. The first and foremost issue is that low-performing employees are not being replaced with better performers. In addition, without turnover there is no mobility upwards in the organization: high-performing, high-potential managers leave for other firms that offer more opportunities. Also, without turnover there is minimal intake of new people with new skills and new knowledge. This leads to *organizational stasis*.

As we progress towards the right-hand side of the figure, past the dashed line, a different dynamic kicks in. Past the optimal point, employee turnover becomes too rapid and begins impacting the firm negatively. When employee turnover is too high, it disrupts communication and coordination in the normal flow of operations; the employees who provide the 'institutional memory' are walking out the door and being replaced with new employees who are still learning how the firm operates. The employees with connections to customers, regulators, suppliers and analysts are turning over, which disrupts communication with these important constituencies. The firm is spending too much of its time recruiting new employees and training them, which distracts the team from focusing on their daily work and performing at their peak. Finally, the company's culture and team cohesion can be impacted negatively.

At the optimal point (shown by the dashed line) the firm enjoys the benefits of moderate turnover, where management stability and change are complementary. The management structure is stable, with management continuity, a strong institutional memory, consistent interfaces with key constituencies, manageable recruiting and training costs, and an enduring organization culture. The management team also enjoys the benefits of change, including periodic opportunities for advancement, infusion of higher performing talent with new skills, ideas and energy, and a dynamic culture that brings in talent to fit a changing competitive landscape. An organization with healthy turnover creates a virtuous cycle of employee development. Employees moving up the organization's hierarchy are continually being challenged, developing their skills and accumulating diverse, relevant experiences.

Appropriate measures of good turnover

Properly analyzing good turnover requires collecting many metrics throughout the organization over a long period of time. All of those metrics are important for digging in and identifying issues in different parts of the organization. However, it is difficult to distill the state and health of an organization based on 30 pages of turnover time-series metrics. Fortunately there are metrics that unify many of these measures and provide a current snapshot of many years of turnover behavior. Firms with moderate good turnover over a long period of time develop a healthy *employee experience curve*, as shown below.

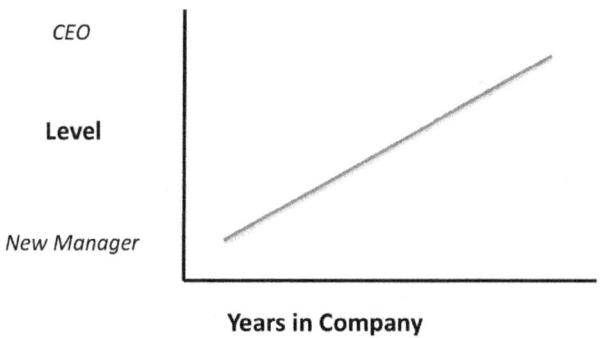

This simple chart shows that managers at the top of the firm have many more years of experience within the firm than newer managers. This seems like a very simple result, given all the complex relationships that go into it, but it is consistent with intuition and experience. Successfully leading a big complex firm through a competitive, global economy requires a diverse set of skills, experiences and network that can be accumulated only through many years of working up through the firm's management hierarchy.

While the result is simple, in practice few firms have this ideal experience curve. Many firms have convoluted curves, which require looking at the component curves of the different divisions, function and regions, which, in turn, require looking at the turnover metrics we described earlier, and sometimes even looking at the metrics for each manager in the organization. Before we dig into curve complexities, let's examine how a firm creates and sustains this experience curve in the presence of constant turnover.

In the beginning of any new company, there is a leader or a small set of leaders. The leader builds the company over a couple of years, hires his/her first employees, the company grows, the employees hire new employees, and so on. Over time, the management structure looks something like the pyramid on the next page. The founding leader is now the CEO, his/her first employees are now the Senior Executives, and the succession of hired employees are now management layers in the organization.

Turnover, Mobility & Talent Upgrading

	Years
CEO	30
Senior Execs	25
Senior Managers	20
Managers Level 2	15
Managers Level 1	10
New Manager	5

So far, this has been a perfectly natural progression, something we read about every day in the business press, and it is consistent with the experience curve we examined on the previous page. However, what happens to this organization and its experience curve over time with good turnover and infusion of external talent? Does the management hierarchy preserve its characteristic of increasing years of experience at the higher levels in the firm, or more simply, does its experience curve keep its same shape?

The answer to these questions is affirmative – if the organization is managing its turnover properly. Even though new employees are being added to the organization continuously, managers at the top of the organization will have more years of experience at the firm than those at the bottom due to promotions and the pyramid shape of management organizations.

The diagram below shows how companies maintain a consistent healthy experience curve. The pyramid on the left is the initial management structure from the previous page. The first column on the left lists the average years of experience within the organization for the managers on that level for a given year (e.g., N = 2011). The middle column computes the average years of experience of those managers through the year, including the impact of turnover. The column on the right lists the average years of experience of those managers the following year (e.g., N+1 = 2012).

For this example, we are assuming personnel change at each level of 10%. At any level in the organization, 90% of the managers don't change and 10% are promoted to the next level or leave the company; these 10% of managers are replaced with managers from the level below them (8%) or by new managers (2%)

Turnover, Mobility & Talent Upgrading

	Years of Experience Within the Organization		
	Year N	Experience after change during the year	Year N+1
CEO	30	30 years*90% + 25 years*8% + 0 years*2% + 1 =	30
Senior Execs	25	25 years*90% + 20 years*8% + 0 years*2% + 1 =	25
Senior Managers	20	20 years*90% + 15 years*8% + 0 years*2% + 1 =	20
Managers Level 2	15	15 years*90% + 10 years*8% + 0 years*2% + 1 =	15
Managers Level 1	10	10 years*90% + 5 years*8% + 0 years*2% + 1 =	10
New Manager	5	5 years*90% + 0 years*10% + 1 =	5

We have not included lateral moves in the calculation because they don't affect the years of experience on any level. The managers on the level below have fewer years of experience than the current level, and the new managers have 0 years of experience in the company. Finally, we add 1 to the calculation to account for the passing of a single year. The left-hand and right-hand columns are identical, which means the experience curve of the organization does not change through time.

Using this approach, we can graph the experience curves for organizations with different turnover rates. As you can see from the figure below, steep slope experience curves spell trouble for an organization. A steep curve on the left-hand side of the figure indicates an organization that has a very high rate of turnover. A steep curve on the right-hand side indicates a very low rate of turnover.

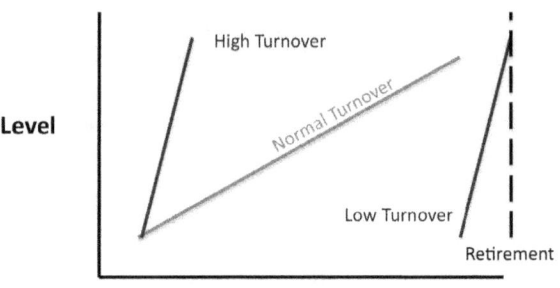

A moderate level of employee turnover alone is not a sure sign of a healthy firm. An average turnover rate may be acceptable, but the average may mask an underlying problem. For example, a seemingly acceptable annual turnover rate of 15% is not acceptable if it is comprised of 0% turnover in the staff functions and 30% turnover in the sales group, or 0% turnover in Europe and 30% in Asia. It is important that employee turnover is evenly distributed throughout the organization and that it occurs at a moderate rate year after year. Let's look at some examples of employee experience curves.

Below is the experience curve for *Global Enterprises*. Does it look like the experience curve of a healthy company? Not only is it unclear, it is confusing as to what is going on with the curve spiking upward towards the right-hand side. However, by looking at the underlying experience curves, starting with regional curves, you can see how we arrived at this puzzling company curve.

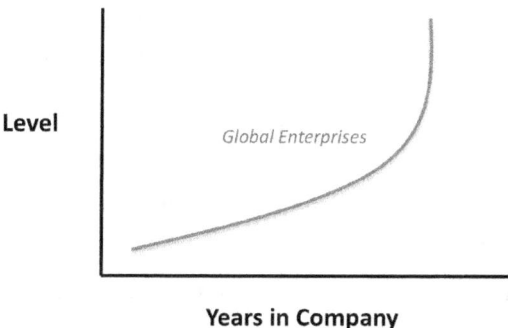

The diagram on the next page shows *Global Enterprise*'s experience curve on the left, and the component curves for its three regions on the right. Now we can see the reason for the strangely upturned curve – an even more oddly shaped curve for the North America division.

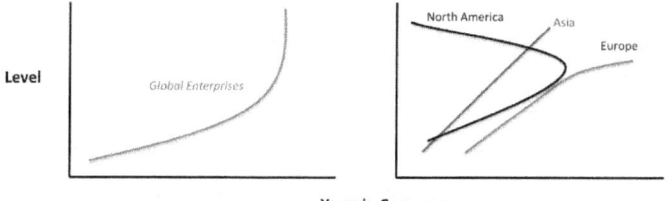

Turnover, Mobility & Talent Upgrading

Global Enterprise's corporate headquarters is in North America. The Board replaced the company's CEO with an outsider, and he recruited his senior team from a rival firm. Now it makes sense. Look at the North America curve, starting from the bottom, and traversing to the top. It begins with a normal experience curve, but then takes a sharp turn left where the senior managers from the rival firm begin averaging into the curve of the existing managers. At the top, on the far left, is the new CEO.

Turning to the other regions, Asia seems to have fairly high turnover and Europe has more normal turnover, but with a strange twist near the longer tenure end of the curve, as shown below.

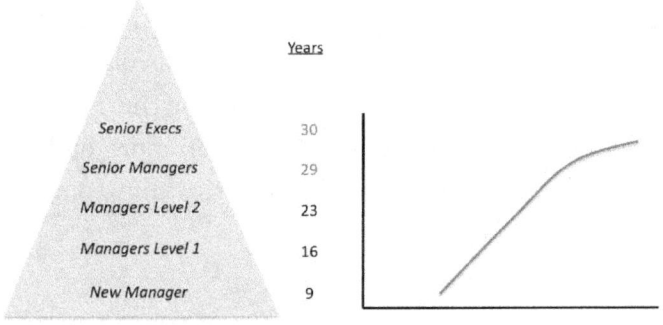

Looking at Europe by organization level, we find that the senior staff there is no longer advancing in the firm, and not being forced to move on to other roles or outside the firm. They have become a bottleneck in management mobility that the company could address by promoting good turnover.

How to encourage good turnover

Good employees may leave a firm for many reasons, including uncompetitive compensation or benefits, excessive workload, bad firm culture, poor morale, lack of advancement opportunities, diminishing status of the firm versus competitors, and industry-related problems, to name a few. The time-tested approaches to managing high turnover include employee satisfaction surveys and associated task forces, exit interviews for departing employees, compensation benchmark studies, and adopting management practices that are being used by companies that are attracting your departing employees.

Excessively low turnover is usually due to a different set of forces. Employees may be too comfortable, even the lowest performing employees. This may be due to a lack of a disciplined performance assessment system, uncompetitive compensation and benefits (i.e., too generous), and the like. If a firm does not have sufficient good turnover, it can be encouraged through mobility planning and talent upgrading.

Mobility

Mobility and good turnover are highly correlated. Good turnover creates opportunities for mobility, and planned proactive mobility leads to good turnover. However, not all mobility is equal. A lack of proactive planned mobility can lead to a rash of reactive unplanned mobility, which can be harmful to a firm.

If done right, mobility is good for the employee and good for the organization. To be good for the employee, mobility to a new position must satisfy some key conditions:

- It should be aligned with the employee's goals,
- The employee should have the skills and experience to succeed in the role, but just barely. That is, the employee must be stretched to succeed,
- The employee should learn new skills, have new experiences, and meet new people, and
- These new skills and knowledge should contribute to the employee's eventual upward mobility.

Mobility can be beneficial to the employee if it is upward (a promotion), lateral, or even downward. The test of good mobility for an employee is whether the employee will be challenged in the new role, and will acquire the skills, experiences and network that immediately or eventually contribute to his or her career advancement.

Good mobility helps the firm in several ways as well. First, if the mobility is good for the employee, then it will lead to a satisfied, striving employee for the foreseeable future. Nothing makes an employee happier than the feeling that the work they are doing is contributing to their advancement. Second, good mobility leads to a steady stream of well-suited employees for openings as they arise. The key to successful internal mobility is understanding and recording each employee's career aspirations and to plan and prepare constantly for mobility to available positions. The tools for mobility analysis are *mobility candidates, mobility chains* and *mobility screening.*

Mobility candidates, as the name implies, are employees who are candidates for filling roles in a firm. In other words, each employee in the firm should have several mobility candidates who could fill their position if they were to leave the firm or move to a different position. The mobility candidates should be judged by the conditions listed previously. For example, if two employees are at the same level, have approximately the same skill set, have the roughly the same performance ratings, have been in their roles for the same amount of time, and both are ready for their next assignment, then one employee is not a good mobility candidate for the other. They each have the requisite skills, but they won't be stretched and they won't learn new skills or have new experiences. It is not enough that a mobility candidate is able to succeed in a role – he/she must also develop in their new role.

Most managers and Personnel departments have an informal or formal system for identifying and listing mobility candidates for each employee, or for employees deemed critical or high risk (for departure). However, less commonly found are organizations that have identified *mobility chains* and associated *strong links*, which are those employees that appear in several mobility chains. As shown below, when an open position is filled it often leads to a chain reaction of internal mobility movements within an organization. A mobility chain is a planning tool that models these movements in advance.

Turnover, Mobility & Talent Upgrading

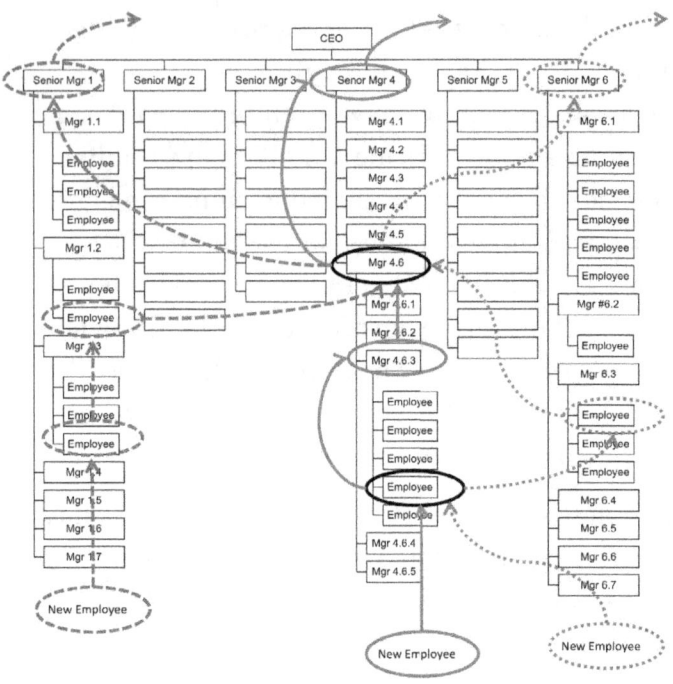

The diagram on above shows mobility chains for three senior managers. If Senior Manager 1 departs, then the best alternative to replace him/her is considered to be Manager 4.6, who would be replaced by an employee reporting to Manager 1.2, and, so on, down to a New Employee. There are similar chains for Senior Manager 4 and 6. If you study these mobility chains it is evident that Manager 4.6 is included in three chains and an employee reporting to Manager 4.6.3 is included in two chains. They are strong performers and they are also strong links in our mobility chains.

Identifying mobility candidates is typically a job for managers and for their Human Resource colleagues. Identifying mobility chains and their strong links is a job for computers and their software. You can see that chains can become a bit complicated for our simple example; they become extremely complicated for an organization of any significant size. Once a strong link is identified, such as Manager 4.6, alternatives need to be identified to ensure that the organization can produce non-intersecting mobility chains for key employees in the organization.

Employees, guided by their Human Resources department, often identify their mobility candidates. Typically each employee lists others in the organization that could take his or her job if the employee were to move to another role. Then the employee's HR generalist reviews the list, may suggest other candidates, and these lists are shared with other HR generalist. This approach may produce non-optimal results if the firm does not have a thorough sourcing process. If the mobility candidates are limited to the employees known by the employee, then there may be exceptional mobility candidates in other parts of the firm that are never put on the list of candidates; mobility screening is a more systematic approach to identifying mobility candidates throughout the firm.

Mobility screening scans the employee hierarchy searching for employees who are candidates for internal mobility. These employees will have been in their current role for sufficient time and they will have consistently high performance ratings. This screening will provoke discussions about the mobility of employees who are overdue for advancement in the organization and are becoming a growing risk for defection to another firm where opportunities for advancement exist. Furthermore, mobility screening may be used to create a mobility chain for a candidate. Used in this manner, mobility screening foreshadows the moves that will likely happen if the firm does not take action proactively.

We have described good turnover, mobility, and the tools for ensuring that good turnover leads to healthy mobility, namely mobility screening, mobility chains and strong link candidates. To set these mobility and turnover processes in motion, we need to create openings in the firm for candidates to move into – this is the role of talent upgrading.

Talent Upgrading

Talent upgrading is the process of identifying employees who are no longer valuable to a company in their current position. Whether an employee should leave the firm or simply move to another position, in either case he/she should vacate their current position.

For successful talent upgrading, companies should have periodic performance evaluations that identify those employees who are not performing satisfactorily and therefore are receiving low performance ratings. In addition, firms should have a rigorous process of reviewing those employees annually and preparing for their eventual removal through mobility planning, which means finding employees who can potentially replace them.

Now we have all the pieces in place for a successful talent management process:

- Rigorous performance evaluations identifying those employees who need to be upgraded,
- Mobility screening to identify potential candidates for positions soon to be vacated,
- Mobility chain planning to ensure that candidates are identified *a priori* for all positions to be filled, and

Turnover, Mobility & Talent Upgrading

- Mobility strong-link candidates are identified, ensuring that several mobility chains do not depend on the same candidate.

When a low performing employee is removed from his/her position, a chain reaction of well-planned employee moves then follow, often leading to an infusion of talent into the firm. Through careful and rigorous planning, we have achieved talent upgrading, internal mobility and good turnover for the benefit of the firm.

Conclusion

Turnover, mobility and talent upgrading are three issues that all companies face periodically. In fact they are closely related processes and should be addressed with a single integrated approach. Disciplined upgrading of talent leads to open positions within a firm; mobility planning leads to a set of career-enhancing employee moves to fill those positions, followed by an infusion of talent into the firm, all of which leads to good turnover, a healthy experience curve, and a virtuous cycle of talent improvement.

Steffen Parratt has 30 years of experience serving a wide range of companies, from small start-ups to large global enterprises. He has a bachelor's and master's degree in mechanical and electrical engineering, respectively, from the University of Rochester, a master's and PhD in engineering from Cornell University, and an MBA from the Wharton School of the University of Pennsylvania.

Notes

[1] Arie C. Glebbeek and Erik H. Bax, "Is High Employee Turnover Really Harmful? An Empirical Test Using Company Records", *The Academy of Management Journal*, April 2004, Vol. 47, No. 2, pp. 277-286.

[2] Harold D. Kohn, "A Test of Abelson and Baysinger's (1984) Optimal Turnover Hypothesis In the Context of Public Organizations Using Computation Simulation", *Research Dissertation*, Virginia Polytechnic Institute and State University, 2008.

[3] Abelson, M., & Baysinger, B., "Optimal and Dysfunctional Turnover: Toward an Organizational Level Model", *Academy of Management Review*, 1984, Vol. 9, No. 2, pp. 331-342.

[4] Society for Human Resource Management (2012). *SHRM 2012-2013 Human Capital Benchmarking Report*.

www.ingramcontent.com/pod-product-compliance
Lightning Source LLC
Chambersburg PA
CBHW070724180526
45167CB00004B/1612